How does it feel?

Child Care from a Parent's Perspective

Anne Stonehouse

_____

Child Care Information Exchange
PO Box 3249 • Redmond, WA 98073
(800) 221-2864
www.ChildCareExchange.com

About the Author

Anne Stonehouse is an early childhood consultant. She was an Associate Professor in the Faculty of Education, Northern Territory University, Darwin, Australia. She has published widely on topics related to the well being of children, and she has a particular professional interest in the complexities, challenges, and critical importance of partnerships between parents and the people who care for their young children. Her publications include *Opening the Doors: Child Care in a Multicultural Society* (Australian Early Childhood Association) and *Prime Times: A Handbook for Excellence in Infant and Toddler Care*, co-authored with Jim Greenman (Redleaf Press, 1996).

ISBN Number:
0-942702-17-4

Publisher:
© Australian Early Childhood Association Inc. (Australia), 1994
© Child Care Information Exchange (USA), 1995, 2003

Design and layout:
Stephanie Williams and Nicki Dunn (Australia)
Sandy and Dennis Brown (USA)
Scott Bilstad and Carole White (USA)

Cartoons:
© mic nic design
The graphic art in this volume was created in Australia and
has been reproduced in its original form.

Cover photograph:
Bonnie Neugebauer

Editors:
P. Windeyer, M. Lamm, S. Gollings, D. Sword (Australia)
Bonnie Neugebauer (USA)

Printed by:
Thomson-Shore, Inc., Dexter, Michigan

Foreword

There is increasing attention in early childhood to the importance of understanding children in the context of their family. Staff in child care centers need to be able to see things from the perspective of parents to thus deepen their understanding of the family context.

Anne Stonehouse in this book asks *"how would you feel if you were a parent when . . ."* and so challenges the reader to look at situations arising in child care from the perspective of a parent.

Parent involvement and participation has been valued as an important aspect of child care. The author offers us an analysis of these concepts and asserts the importance of moving to partnerships based on mutual respect, equality, and sensitivity.

This book is an extension of early work by Anne Stonehouse on the interactions of staff and parents and provides both a theoretical and practical basis for re-looking at partnerships from another point of view — the parents'!

Tonia Godhard, President
Australian Early Childhood Association

contents

1. introduction

We are all assisted in our relationships, whether personal or professional, by seeing situations from the perspective of others. What this book aims to do, with the complex relationships that exist between teachers and parents of the children they care for, is to help staff get a clearer idea of how child care feels to a parent. Some of the material that follows will hopefully give you some new insights; some of it will no doubt be a reminder of what you really already know but have lost sight of in your busy, complex role.

Increasingly in children's services, there is recognition of the importance of understanding the child in the context of family and culture, and of taking into account the preferences, values, needs, and wishes of parents. Parents are the most important people in a child's life. People who work in early childhood programs[1] cannot replace parents, even in the 2,500 hours annually that a child might spend in care. Furthermore, parents don't want to be replaced. We need to have a clear view of our early childhood programs as supplementing and complementing

---

[1] The terms *teacher* and *caregiver* in this publication are used for staff in both center and home-based settings. The term *program* refers to the daily experience offered for children and their families in both settings.

1

the lessons children learn in other parts of their lives. We need to understand that no matter what age the child is currently or upon entry into care, no matter how long the daily separations, parents are not on the periphery, but at the heart of what matters to their child. Caldwell (1984) said it well:

> Professional child care is not a substitute or a competitor for parental care. To some extent, professional child care represents a version of the extended family which has adapted to the social realities of the modern world. (p. 4)

Looking at the child in context means acknowledging cultural background, and accepting the culture bound nature of what we know about child development and what we believe about best practice with children.

In addition, we have a responsibility to let parents know about their critical role, because they may not be fully aware of it. Teachers can nurture a robust, healthy relationship between parent and child. We know from research done in the last ten or fifteen years about the importance of this relationship for a child's later development. Teachers can play a major role in shaping for parents a positive picture of their child, a focus on his or her individuality and unique strengths. Relationships between parents and teachers, perhaps more so than the activities and experiences offered to children, are likely to be a major determinant of the long term impact on children of participation in early childhood programs.

An additional reward is that the more parents understand and respect the work you do as a teacher, the more likely it is that they will be effective advocates for early childhood programs and for the profession.

Along with increasing recognition of the importance of parent-staff partnerships, there is also increasing recognition that establishing and maintaining partnerships is a very hard thing to do, much harder than simply looking at children, to use Rita Warren's (1977) words, as though they "spring into being each morning when they come to us and dematerialize at their departure" (p. 8). When the child is viewed in the context of her or his family situation, it is harder to decide what is best.

An example:

A parent requests that her almost three year old be kept awake in the afternoon so that he will go to sleep earlier in the evening. This is a child who acts tired and sleepy after lunch. A *decontextualized child* approach, looking only at the situation from the perspective of the child's developmental needs, makes it easy to refuse the request as not being in the best interests of the child. Taking a *child in the context of family* approach requires you to take into account the fact that his mother, the only parent at home, is studying for a training course to enable her to gain employment, and as it is nearing the end of the semester, she has a number of assignments due and examinations to prepare for. A judgment about what is best for the child in the long run is not so easy when taking into account this information.

If teachers are being honest, they will say that the hardest thing about working with children is working with the children's parents. It is hard mainly because it is complex, but it is also hard for at least four other reasons:

> lack of appreciation for the importance of the work,
>
> lack of attention or superficial treatment in pre-service courses and in-service education,

inadequate acknowledgment of demands on staffing, and therefore budgets,

staff resistance to and discomfort with relinquishing a view of themselves as *experts*.

It is hoped that this book will provide a basis for talking over issues in family day care homes, child care programs, and after school programs.

2. what is a partnership? how can we help create one?

The term used to describe the relationship that should exist is *partnership*. Parent-teacher partnerships in child care share most of the characteristics of partnerships in other areas, in business and in personal relationships. What follows is an exploration of some of the characteristics of parent-teacher partnerships.

Mutual respect

Respect is an essential ingredient of partnership; if it is missing, there is no hope of a partnership. Respect for parents is easy to pay lip service to but very difficult to put into action in the work place, especially in relation to parents who are difficult, demanding, irresponsible, and those whom teachers believe are not doing the right thing by their child. You have to acknowledge and deal with your prejudices and biases.

Teachers may need help to examine their own prejudices. We all have them, but we may often be blind to them. It helps to discuss with other staff individual and collective notions of the ideal parent, the *pain in the neck* parent. Once these issues are out in the open, questions can be asked about where these views come from. To what extent do they come from our investment in the *correctness* of our own cultural background and lifestyle?

Trust

Learning to trust takes time. Like love at first sight, immediate trust between a teacher and a parent may happen occasionally, but mostly trust comes from honest, open communication, compromise, and negotiation.

Staff who work hard to form partnerships with parents sometimes feel frustrated, even offended, that parents don't seem to trust them right away. It doesn't matter how good *you* know you are, it takes time for parents to know this.

While trust cannot be hurried, it can be nurtured. For trust to happen, each partner has to believe that the other is doing the best she or he can, another belief easier stated than put into practice.

Sensitivity to the perspective of the other

Parenting is not easy these days, if it ever was. Some would say it is harder now, partly because of higher expectations and more responsibilities competing with the parenting role.

There is so much advice for parents, some conflicting, some the simplistic *this works for all situations* type. Parents who use child care have the extra pressure of having little Johnny and Janie, and therefore themselves as parents, under the scrutiny of professionals. It has been said that sending your child off to child care is like opening up your drawers and cupboards for inspection by professional house cleaners, except it is worse because at least there is a direct relationship between your input into your drawers and cupboards and the result.

That is, you can control the condition of your drawers and cupboards! People who are new to parenting are especially vulnerable, as they may lack confidence about their parenting skills.

In addition, some parents will be enthusiastic and confident about using early childhood services, and many will be ambivalent. Some will be using child care because they have no other choice; they would much prefer to be at home with their children. Avoid making the generalization that most parents are either *happy to just "dump" their children in care* or *consumed by guilt*. Rather, as you get to know parents, you will learn about their attitudes toward using care. These attitudes will be a major factor in their relationship and communication with you.

Although a source of frustration, teachers have to accept that parents typically won't be able to see the big picture the way you do. Their main interest, as it should be, is "How does this affect my child?" Staff must accept the inevitable tension that comes from the difference between parents' perspectives and their own.

Every child needs a strong advocate, at least one person who is crazy about him or her. A request made by a parent on behalf of the child may be ill founded or impossible to accommodate, but making the request is a parent acting as an advocate.

Ongoing open *both ways* communication

A silent drop off or pick up of a child by parents with no exchange of information makes it inevitable that the experience in the program and in the home are not linked. This can be confusing for the child. It means that teachers and parents are operating with less than a full picture of the child. It may mean that, over time, parents feel less involved, less central in their child's life. Working in parallel or in opposition certainly does not constitute a partnership or the basis for one. Ensuring that the parent, as well as the child, is greeted genuinely at the beginning and end of the day is an important step toward ongoing communication.

Common goals that are clear and agreed on

Parents want what is best for their child. Mostly they want the same things for their children that we do: to live a fulfilled life, to do well in school and at work, and to have positive relationships with other people. But parents have different values, and they may also have different views of how to achieve those aims for their child.

Furthermore, they may not have the skills and knowledge that come from years of early childhood study and experience.

Equally important, they don't have the objectivity that teachers and other staff have about their child, the objectivity that sometimes contributes to sound judgment. You could say that the problem with parents is that they care about their children.

Teamwork: absence of rivalry or competition

Rita Warren (1977), writes that child saving is the "number one occupational hazard" of people who work with other people's children (p. 8). When we start to see ourselves as doing a better job with children than their parents, we are on the way to becoming harsh critics of, or competitors with, parents. Janet Gonzalez-Mena describes it as a "savior complex," when teachers see their role as rescuing children from their parents (p. 213).

All teachers should examine their own attitudes about parents who work outside the home when their children are young. A strong belief that every parent who possibly can should stay home with their child while he or she is young can really get in the way of forming a partnership with parents who have chosen not to be full time parents at home and to leave their child or children in care.

Equality: fairly equal distribution of power

Teachers sometimes feel intimidated by parents, and parents sometimes feel intimidated by teachers. Each may feel the other has the upper hand in the relationship. Signals are misread when this is not acknowledged. Parents are the customers or clients of your service, and power comes with that status. However, when it comes to forming a partnership, the ball's in your court. As the professional, you have the upper hand.

Recognition and valuing of the unique contribution and strengths of the partner

If teachers are being honest with themselves, they may confess that they are comfortable involving parents as long as parents defer to their professional judgment and are prepared to go along with what they know is best. It's much easier to involve parents when all of them have the right ideas, that is, *your ideas*, and when they don't try to rock the boat.

Early childhood professionals are sometimes very critical of parents because they don't know what we know, but why should they?

We have studied for a number of years, and we believe that our profession is complex, sophisticated, and requires considerable knowledge and lots of skills. It is silly to think that just anyone can understand or even appreciate the things we do. At the same

time, if partnerships with parents are the aim, ways of sharing professional knowledge with them must be found.

What do parents and teachers contribute to the partnership? Parents are the experts on their child, they have biographical information, insights, and knowledge that are very useful. They also have a lifelong investment in the child, which affects their perspective. Teachers, on the other hand, contribute experience of many children, which helps them to see each individual child in a broader context. Most experienced teachers, in other words, have *seen it all* when it comes to children, and this allows them to be more dispassionate and objective about a particular child.

Shared decision making

Making decisions together about the child is the cornerstone of partnerships. Even when teachers feel perfectly capable of

making a decision on their own, they should resist the urge. Parents who trust teachers may be willing to let them make decisions — because of their own feelings of inadequacy as parents, the other demands and pressures in their lives, a belief that this is the expectation of the staff, and a desire to avoid appearing meddlesome or mistrusting of staff. Helping the child learn to use the toilet, moving a child from one group to another, adding new foods to a baby's diet, or dealing with a persistent behavior problem are just some of the many situations where shared decision making is appropriate.

Remember!
Shared decision making is *not* a matter of informing parents of a decision you as caregiver have made!

3. what partnership is not

Partnership is not the same as parent involvement or parent participation.

A parent-staff partnership in an early childhood setting is a matter of spirit, of attitude, and cannot be measured by participation or involvement by parents in the work of the early childhood program. Partnerships do not rest on parent *involvement* in the program, but on communication, decision making systems, and daily interactions that promote shared decision making and mutual trust.

The aim of our relationship with parents is a partnership to foster closer feelings of belonging. Inevitably programs that have a partnership with parents do have in place a number of ways that parents can assist and contribute, but that is not sufficient. It is possible to have in place a number of ways for parents to help out, and not have a partnership. On the other hand, it is possible to have a partnership with a parent who does not contribute or get involved with the institution. To date, most early childhood professionals have been better at involving parents than at forming partnerships with them.

Early childhood professionals, all of us, need to move away from measuring the extent of relationships with parents by attendance at meetings, the profits from a fund raising activity, whether the board of directors or parent committee has a full complement of members, or even, I would suggest, how many parents *help out* in the rooms. It is well documented in the literature about parent involvement in schools that what parents want is a relationship with the teacher, that is, with the person or persons who work closely with their child. No doubt this is what parents of children in child care want too. But, by and large, the ways devised to date for parents to be involved are more likely to give them a link with the *institution* rather than a direct means of forming a relationship with the *person or people who work with their child*.

It's really hard not to think more favorably about the *involved* parents than the *uninvolved*, but this is to be avoided. Involvement should be viewed as welcomed and appreciated, but optional. Relying on involvement or participation in the life of the center as the means of forming relationships with parents means that some parents are left out because they cannot be available, and others are frustrated either because they feel pressure to help out in order to be seen as *good* parents, or they feel there is no way they can meet expectations.

Partnership is not the same with everybody

Each partnership will be unique. Some parents will seek out information more actively, ask more questions, appear more interested, offer more information about the child, divulge information more freely about their lives and circumstances, as well as be much more involved in the life of the program than others. As is true of our relationships with children, individual differences are to be respected and accepted.

Just as children should be viewed as individuals, so should parents. Teachers should resist the temptation to lapse into generalizations based on culture, or about parents in general:

> "What do you expect; he's a single parent."
>
> "Typical, all Greeks overdress their children."
>
> "I wonder why these yuppie two career couples bother to have children — they don't spend any time with them."
>
> "They don't appreciate us; they all think we are just baby sitters."

Parents of babies may have special needs. They may be less certain that putting their child in care is the right thing, as use of child care for very young children is more controversial than use for older, preschool-aged children. Secondly, there is not as much choice of care for very young children, so parents have more investment in making the care arrangement work and more anxiety about what happens if it doesn't work. Thirdly, the child is more vulnerable, more dependent, more at the mercy of teachers to notice their indications of need. Fourthly, parents are likely to be less experienced and less confident. And lastly, parents of babies are likely to be very tired much of the time.

Partnership is not the same as becoming friends

While friendships may emerge between parents and teachers, a partnership is a professional relationship. In fact, personal friendships can cause problems of perceived favoritism, confidentiality, and conflicts of interest, and should be approached with caution. Particularly in family day care, caring for the children of people who are already friends may make it particularly challenging to establish a professional *business* relationship with the parents. This should be discussed thoroughly with prospective parents before they begin care.

4. through a parent's eyes

Following are some common situations that occur when parents use child care. Some of these elaborate on points already made.

🍎 *how would you feel if you were a parent when . . .*

**you get a message at work:
"PLEASE CALL YOUR CHILD CARE CENTER"?**

You get a sinking feeling in the pit of your stomach. You are *not* likely to think "Oh boy, I wonder what good news they want to share with me now." There's that same feeling if you get a message that the director wants to see you: it's not going to be good news.

On the other hand, what a solidly good feeling it is if the teacher at the end of the day has some *good news* for you about your child; an accomplishment, an interest, an experience she or he enjoyed.

Make it a priority to share with parents all the good news you can. Parents love hearing anything that demonstrates someone else's pleasure, delight, and pride in their child. Most parents want to know, but are not likely to ask:

"Does my child measure up?"
"Do you like my child?"
"Do you notice my child during the day?"

Parents are pleased to get information, but more importantly, your good news is a sign that their child is *known* to the people or person he or she spends the days with. One parent said, "The thing I like is that they made me feel that my child is the most special one in the center, and yet I know that they make other parents feel that way too" (Stonehouse, 1991, p. 28).

🍎 *how would you feel if you were a parent when . . .*

the teacher excitedly tells you about a developmental first that happened, or refers to your child as "my baby"?

Most parents are ambivalent about the special relationship between you and their child. They know it's important, and they are pleased when their child is happy and secure. They really wouldn't want it to be any other way, but they do not want to be replaced in their child's affections. I heard a parent say once, "I want Melanie's caregiver to be the *second* most important person in her life — after me." Another parent said, "It isn't just that they are reporting to me. They give me the feeling that they are devoted to my child, but always there is the clear message that *I* am my child's most important person."

Expressions of delight in a child or feelings of caring and attachment must be tempered with understanding that you are in no way competing with the parent for the child's affections.

The times when you see parents, at the beginning and end of the day, are not parents' best times. The mornings are likely to be rushed; parents have already rushed to get there. In the late afternoon parents are tired and anticipating the hectic time ahead of them at home. They may be particularly vulnerable and sensitive at those times.

It is generally agreed that it is best to save news about *firsts*, such as walking, talking, and other significant milestones, for parents to discover for themselves. Even though parents may subconsciously know that you have probably seen it first, mostly they appreciate being allowed to discover it for themselves.

❦ *how would you feel if you were a parent when . . .*

you bring your child in and no one greets you and receives your child, or when your presence is acknowledged only superficially and/or at a distance?

Being received by a teacher, welcomed, and helped to settle in is important for the child to help make the transition from parent to teacher, from home to care. Even when the child is not distressed, both parent and child need the feeling of being welcomed and their presence acknowledged. Perhaps you can recall the unsettling feeling of entering a group and your presence not being acknowledged by others. Parents have stressed being greeted personally and received as contributing significantly to feelings of trust. A parent of a baby, when asked to identify what made him feel confident about leaving his baby in care, mentioned first and with no hesitation, "I never had to just put her down and leave; someone always took her."

23

Of course, help when the child is upset is even more important:

🍂 *how would you feel if you were a parent when . . .*

you are already late for work;
you bring your child in;
other children are playing happily together;
your child is firmly attached to your leg,
screaming?

Many parents, at times such as these, feel:

Guilt: "I'm sure I'm ruining her for life by leaving her. My mother is probably right. I should have stayed home with her until she goes to school."

Ineptness: "Help, what do I do *now*?"

Desperation: "As soon as I can pry her off my leg, or if she shuts her eyes, I'll just bolt out of here as fast as I can and let them handle it."

Frustration: "Why can't *my* child be as well behaved as other children?"

Doubts: "What's so horrible about this place that makes her so upset to be here?"

All of these feelings are natural, and this is a time when professional help from a teacher is most needed. Obviously, if the child is very new, fear is normal; and, whenever possible, it is best for all concerned if parents spend some time with the child in the new place helping her or him settle. However, this situation can happen when a child has been coming to care for a long time and seemingly *out of the blue*, for no apparent reason. This is a time when it is crucial for the teacher to help both child and parent. If the parent can stay around, this may be advisable and will help in some cases, but it may not in others. The act of separating from people you love, even when you know they will come back, and even when you are being left with people who know you and care about you, can be painful.

Without being callous, when it is time for the parent to go, the teacher will need to be her most supportive, warm, and comforting self with the child, while at the same time helping the parent say goodbye and leave. Sneaking away without saying goodbye may look like a very attractive short term solution, tempting in that it allows the parent to avoid the pain of leaving a distressed child. Caregivers may need to help parents see that *sneaking away without saying goodbye is never a good idea*, as it undermines feelings of trust and security. Encourage the parent to call or offer to call them to let them know when the child has settled. Reassure the parent that this behavior is normal for some children.

🍎 *how would you feel if you were a parent when . . .*

**the teacher says,
"Don't worry, she'll be fine as soon as you leave?"**

This comment is frequently made to reassure parents as they part from their distressed child. It is worth thinking about the possible interpretations parents may make, and to minimize the chance that these are the messages they will get. A common inference made from a child's quick recovery is that the child is *playing a game*, being manipulative, or just plain trying to make things difficult for the parent. Amazingly, these motives are often attributed even to babies! Babies are more clever than we give them credit for, but not *that* clever! A quick recovery does not necessarily mean that the expression of pain and distress was not genuine. Many of us actually behave very similarly, crying as the loved one goes through the door at the airport to get on the plane, but recovering before we get back to our car.

Unfortunately, even when the most sensitive procedures are followed to help a child feel secure in care, the child may still be distressed at the time of separation. This makes it no less important to do all we can to help the child, but parents must not think that if they choose the optimum time and the perfect way to depart, the child will happily see them to the door and wave goodbye.

More concerning, a parent could infer from the message above that it is their presence that is causing the distress, and that, once in the hands of competent professionals, the child will quickly recover. Many parents who use child care may be prone to interpreting your comments to suggest lack of competence on their part or denial of their special place in their child's life.

Leaving a child who is distressed is painful for most parents, and they need as much support and reassurance as the child does. Reminding the parent that the child's behavior is normal, helping them to leave when the time is right, and encouraging them to phone to see how their child is later on will help the parent to leave feeling more secure.

🍂 *how would you feel if you were a parent when . . .*

your child is happy and settled, but you feel ambivalent about leaving?

Some parents do a kind of "Dame Nellie's farewell," leaving and reappearing, or threatening to leave, almost as though they want to see the child acknowledge their departure with distress.

It is normal for some parents to have separation problems, even when their child does not. This phenomenon manifests itself most powerfully when a child goes off to high school. If we parents had our wishes, we would probably go with them, holding their hands! Avoiding critical judgments of such parents requires professionalism, and helping parents acknowledge their feelings requires sensitivity.

Whether children are distressed or happy, parents need help knowing when and how to leave, and appreciating the importance of definiteness about leaving for their child's well being. This is a key time for the focus of the teacher's skill, sensitivity, and concern to extend beyond the child to encompass the parent as well.

🍎 *how would you feel if you were a parent when . . .*

staff always seem too busy to talk to you?

Both parents and teachers often report the other being too busy to talk as an obstacle to partnership. Parents and staff *are* busy, especially at the times of day they usually see one another. Some parents who may appear uninterested in talking with you may, in fact, be responding to the fact that you appear to be so busy that they don't want to take up your time. A partnership must be built on frequent, sometimes brief, interchanges backed up with written communication and an atmosphere of openness and respect.

🍂 *how would you feel if you were a parent when . . .*

**you have been up all night with another child
who is ill with a flu that has been through the whole family;
you bring in your child with her hair uncombed,
holding onto a cold piece of toast; once there,
you realize that you have forgotten
to bring the required change of clothes?**

Parents are people like us, struggling to do the right thing in a busy, sometimes confusing, world. They have multiple roles. They are spouses, workers, sons, and daughters; and these responsibilities inevitably mean that they cannot and should not put their child's needs first *right now*. On the other hand, staff are there for the child only, and it is easy to become critical when parents do not appear to be putting the child first. Given their multiple roles, they cannot and should not always do so.

🍎 *how would you feel if you were a parent when . . .*

**you return to pick up your child and,
instead of seeming glad to see you,
he hardly acknowledges your return,
acts up, or, worse still,
resists leaving to go home?**

This very common situation can be one of the critical incidents in
both parent/child relationships and the parent/caregiver
partnership. It can be seen over and over in early childhood
programs, and happens like this: The parent returns after a hard
day's work, hoping for an affectionate, warm welcome from their
child and a relaxed departure from care. Instead of the warm
welcome, the child looks up briefly, makes a superficial
acknowledgment, and returns his attention to what he was
doing. The message is clearly, "Oh, hello Dad, you're back. No

big deal — I'll just continue doing what I'm doing." Or the child appears to see the parent's return as a cue to break every rule about acceptable behavior. Or, worst of all, the child actively resists leaving to go home.

In all cases, the parent may think, "Well, it's happened, he doesn't think I'm anything special, he doesn't even like me any more." In the case of the child resisting going home, the parent may also infer that it means that the child prefers the teacher to the parent, the center or the family day care home to his own home. The teacher's role in these situations is to provide alternative explanations that will be reassuring to the parent; and there are a number. Firstly, parents need to know that, as unpleasant as they are, these situations are fairly common, and that, except in rare and extreme circumstances, they never mean that parents have been replaced in the affections of their child. Some alternative explanations follow:

In the case of the minimal greeting, although no parent would prefer a greeting like this, it is actually a positive sign. The child is saying through his actions that he knew Daddy would return, that Daddy has in fact returned; and while he is happy to see him, his return is not a big deal. If you think about it, that is the way most older children and adults greet people after routine absences. It is actually a sign that the child feels secure.

The child for whom the sight of the parent is a signal to turn on his worst behavior is probably doing one of two things. Young children often ask through their behavior questions they cannot ask in words. The child may be asking, "I wonder who is in charge here. This is an interesting situation, where there are two people who *take charge* of me, redirect me, stop me. I wonder who will do it when they are together?" A second possibility is that the sight of the parent is a trigger for the child to let down his defenses, to feel the way he really feels at the end of a long, busy day with other children. It takes a lot of stamina and resilience for a young child (just as it does for an adult!) to cope with being in a group all day. Seeing that person whom you love and who you know will love you no matter how horrible you act is a cue to act as tired and grouchy as you actually feel. Again, this is not very different to the way many of us behave, even though we have more self control and a greater sense of what is appropriate behavior. During a difficult day when we feel lousy, we may be on our best behavior at work, very professional. But once we get home and are with those people who will put up with us no matter what, we *let it all hang out* and act as lousy as we feel. So, acting up may be just a tired child's way of saying "I've had it!"

Many teachers, as well as parents, misinterpret a child resisting going home at the end of the day. It is important to recognize, first of all, that these are often the same children who protest at being left in the morning. That suggests one possible interpretation: simply that children may resist change if they are happy where they are. A child at the end of the day may simply be happy doing what he is doing, and he does not want to be abruptly extracted from it. He may be saying, "Just a minute, don't rush me, I'm in the middle of something important." Sometimes the child is saying, again in his actions because he can't say it in words, "Stop here a while, I want you to spend some time in this place that is special to me," just as we adults want people we are fond of to see where we work, where we live. Sometimes the resistance may be a bit of payback, the child saying, "I didn't like you leaving me this morning, so I am not going to go easily now." It has also been suggested that children, being almost always wiser than we give them credit for, may be thinking about the hectic and not very pleasant time that awaits them between arriving at home and going to bed, and they may be voting with their feet to stay in this more child-centered place!

🍎 *how would you feel if you were a parent when . . .*

you take time off to help out in the classroom and you feel as though your time is being wasted, or that the staff have had to come up with something to keep you busy?

Many parents feel the need to conform with whatever appear to be the institutional expectations in order to be perceived as a *good* parent.

Identifying a variety of ways that parents can feel connected to the program is important; and one of those ways is through making an authentic contribution to the operation of the center by using skills, interests, and talents. These ways should range from simpler contributions, such as donating junk materials, to what could be termed more sophisticated contributions, such as participation on the board of directors or use of specialist expertise. It is critical that all contributions be valued equally and, as has been said frequently, that parents not be judged on the quantity or quality of their contributions.

Hendrick (1988) warns us about restricting parent involvement to menial tasks:

> Over and over I have witnessed teachers asking mothers to wipe off tables or help in the kitchen or letting them simply stand around, smiling a lot, but knowing in their hearts their time in being wasted. [They] may prefer simple tasks in the beginning because they are familiar, not threatening, and because they do not want to make waves or antagonize the teacher. However, keeping them at such tasks is fundamentally denigrating, teaches children that parents are not important . . . , and deprives children of the unique contribution such people can make if properly acknowledged. (p. 261)

🐦 *how would you feel if you were a parent when . . .*

you are identified and greeted by the staff only as "Michael's mom"?

Parents are people; they have names. As discussed previously, they have an identity other than being the parent of the child you care for.

🐦 *how would you feel if you were a parent when . . .*

you hand your child over to someone that you, and she, do not know very well, if at all?

This is an especially significant issue for people with young babies, who are very vulnerable and who have few ways of indicating that they are satisfied with the care they receive. High staff turnover in centers and rotating shifts make it difficult to maintain consistent communication with parents by having the same person talk to them at the beginning and end of the day. Directors should recognize the importance of consistency of care for both children and parents and give this priority in staffing arrangements. Certainly when a child and parent are new, it is crucial that there be one person designated as the main caregiver for the child, and therefore the major communicator with the parent.

Again, it takes time and lots of communication to get to know the other person and to bring about trust.

❦ *how would you feel if you were a parent when . . .*

**you describe your toddler's uncooperative behavior
at home, and the caregiver says,
"No, we haven't seen anything
like that here; she's very cooperative"?**

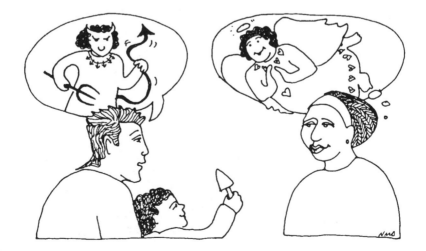

Parents need to be reminded by us of the truth in the song lyrics "You always hurt the ones you love, the ones you shouldn't hurt at all." Children almost always behave better for other people than they do for their parents. It is easy in our efforts to reassure parents about their child to inadvertently undermine their feelings of competence as parents. This, by the way, is also a partial explanation for *going to pieces* behavior at the end of the day, discussed previously.

🍃 *how would you feel if you were a parent when . . .*

there is a significant change in your child's daily experience, for example, she is moved to another group; her main caregiver leaves and is replaced; or toilet training is started and you haven't been informed of or consulted about the decision?

Parents can easily feel left out of their child's day. Even when caregivers feel perfectly capable of making a decision about the child, it should be made in collaboration with parents.

Periodically, policies and, more importantly, practices with parents should be put under the microscope. Ask yourself how you involve parents in decision making. One useful exercise is to make up a chart with three columns labeled as follows:

No Compromise (that is, the "Sacreds," the areas where, because of your philosophy, policies or regulations, there can be no comprise)	Shared Decision Making with Parents	Parents' Decisions

Make a list of what situations fit under each heading. If the middle list is not the longest, some critical analysis of your practices may be necessary. Ask yourselves what are the reasons behind the items you put in the No Compromise column. Are they valid? Are they in the best interests of children in the context of their families?

It is not easy to strike the best balance between adopting best professional practice and responding to parents' requests and priorities. Some programs, wanting to empower parents, seem to adopt an *anything goes* philosophy that results in efforts to negotiate everything with parents and accommodate individual parents' wishes, at the expense of the quality of the experience for all. It is as though the staff abrogate professional knowledge and expertise. A more common and equally unsatisfactory stance is one that gives a clear message to parents that "we know what

is best, we will tell you; if you don't like it, go somewhere else."
As is true with most things, there is a sensible position in
between. Convey clearly the following:

that requests and expressions of concern by parents are
always taken seriously,

that there are channels for raising concerns,

the program's philosophies and policies,

the areas where there is little or no choice because of
philosophy, policies, or regulations.

🍃 *how would you feel if you were a parent when . . .*

you go to a parent and staff social occasion where it feels as if everyone except you knows someone else, OR no one among the staff or families is from your cultural background or speaks your first language?

Most of us have had that experience somewhere. A strong feeling of community among parents and staff is a good thing for those that are in the group, but it can have the effect of shutting some people out, making them feel like outsiders. Insiders can have an illusion of themselves as a friendly inclusive group, but it may feel that way only to those who are already on the inside.

Parents new to a program will always take a while to feel comfortable; but when cultural and language differences are added to the picture, parents' discomfort and their concerns about their child's well being escalate. These feelings are heightened when the use of care by non family members is one that is foreign to the parent and not part of their culture of origin.

Early childhood programs should aim to reflect in their staff the diversity of current users or, better still, the diversity that exists in the local community. Experience shows that having staff from a particular cultural group encourages families from that cultural group to use the center.

It may not be possible to reflect every group, but a program that demonstrates comfort with diversity will create an atmosphere where no one feels different because everyone is different! Familiar people, objects, language, music, and foods throughout the care environment help parents feel comfortable and secure as well as contributing to a good quality care environment for children.

🍎 *how would you feel if you were a parent when . . .*

**you overhear a teacher telling a parent how wonderful their
child is, how much pleasure she gives the staff. For
example, saying to another parent, "Your José is just the
cleverest child; he talks so well for a two year old"
— while your own child is still using single words?**

Many teachers, if they are honest, will confess to having favorites
among the children. That is, if someone said to them, "Choose a
child from the group to take home and be yours," most teachers
could comply. Similarly, many could also identify the child they
would be *least* likely to choose. This is only human nature.
However, professional behavior dictates that it must *never* be
apparent to anyone which child is the favorite or the least
favorite. Parents, always on the lookout for evidence that their
child is liked and highly thought of, will be prone to noticing

actual evidence of favoritism or inferring favoritism. Fortunately, such is human nature that different types of children (and parents, for that matter!) appeal to different teachers.

❦ how would you feel if you were a parent when . . .

you've had a hard day at work and, when you come to pick up your child, you are told that she bit three children today. You are asked if there has been anything happening at home that may have contributed to this?

Two points need to be made here. It has been stressed previously that teachers should share all the good news they can with parents. They need to be more careful and tactful when it comes to *not so good* news. For some parents on some days, unpleasant news about their child's behavior may be the last straw. Without being directly dishonest, teachers can dilute the bad news, be selective about what they convey, or save it for another time.

The second issue stems from a natural human tendency to blame the other. Let's confess: parents usually get the blame but not the credit. What is the first thing most teachers would say when two year old Susan starts biting any exposed flesh she has access to or ten month old Juan won't settle down to sleep, or one year old Carla screams when her mom leaves in the morning? "I wonder if something is going on at home."

I can honestly report that I have never heard an early childhood professional say in such a circumstance, "I wonder if there is something about me or about our program that is troubling the child?" And parents are no different. Undesirable behavior in their child is almost always assumed to have been picked up in care.

The healthiest way to approach problem behavior is with a sense of shared responsibility by the parent and the teacher and the will to work together to solve the problem.

🍎 *how would you feel if you were a parent when . . .*

**your child's teacher says that she is at her wits end
with your child — that she is ready to give up?**

Usually, as was said before, experienced teachers have seen
everything when it comes to children's behavior, and they know
that difficult behavior in a child can be dealt with, or, if not, that
it will pass eventually. Occasionally, however, teachers feel truly
baffled and defeated by a child's behavior, ready to give up. This
may happen more frequently in family day care, where there is
no relief continually at hand to deal with difficult behavior. It is
critically important when discussing the problem with parents to
convey what I call *honesty with optimism*. Parents want you to be
honest with them about their child, but professionalism dictates
that this honesty should be tempered with a positive expectation

of resolution of the problem. Situations where parents are asked to find other care should be rare, and must be handled with tact and sensitivity, as parents are very likely to get the message that you have given up on their child.

🍎 *how would you feel if you were a parent when . . .*

another parent asks you how old your child is and expresses surprise that he/she isn't walking, talking, using the toilet, etc.?

It is a mixed blessing that participation in group situations gives parents the opportunity to compare their child with others about the same age. Teachers should continually celebrate individuality and help parents to see the particular strengths their child has. Most children have them; it's just that some are more obvious than others. For example, early walking is much more obvious than advanced skill in using hands and fingers, and yet the latter is just as exciting and important in terms of the assistance it gives the child in exploring the world.

A range of developmental milestones should be highlighted as they occur, but with little emphasis on when they occur. After all, how many of us believe that our lives have been affected one way or the other by when we learned to use the toilet, first walked, or uttered our first word!

Moving from one group to another (for example, out of the infant room, into the toddler room) is usually interpreted by parents as a sign of achievement by the child, and transferring a child is in fact often based on indications of readiness as assessed by the staff. If your child is the last to move up, or the oldest in the group where younger children have moved, you may see this as a sign that the child is not quite *up to scratch.* Teachers need to take care to explain movement or lack thereof and, again, to emphasize the special qualities and strengths of each child.

Parents can't help but wonder how their child measures up. Our communication with parents needs to help them appreciate the unique strengths of their child and avoid excessive comparisons with others.

how would you feel if you were a parent when . . .

you are contacted to come and pick up your child who is sick?

A sick child in care places extra stress not only on that child, but on the teachers and other children as well. When a child becomes obviously unwell in care, staff can be resentful, making it is easy to lapse into parent bashing: "I guess she couldn't be bothered staying home with him" or "Isn't it awful the way parents just dump their kids and expect us to look after them when they're sick?" It isn't always easy to decide whether or not a child is sick enough to stay home. It isn't always easy to take a day off work. It isn't always easy to find alternate care. It isn't always easy to predict if the child will get better or worse during the day. While a few parents may appear to be callous when it comes to leaving a sick child, most parents are well meaning and try to do the right thing. Often the parent who is called to pick up a sick child feels guilty anyway, without staff adding to it.

🦋 *how would you feel if you were a parent when . . .*

**the caregiver doesn't listen to you or
your requests are rejected out of hand?**

Staff often complain that parents don't listen to them. Parents complain about the same thing. Every child in care needs a strong advocate, and that advocate is the parent. It has been stated previously that parents are to some extent *one-eyed*, and so they should be. That is, they see everything from the perspective of *How will this affect my child and me?* This has to be accepted by staff. While it is not possible to accede to every request a parent makes, and some of their requests will be quite unreasonable from your perspective, it is important to view these requests as parents acting as they should. And when there is a difference in what a parent wants and what staff see as appropriate or possible, instead of immediately moving into "This is what we do here" *power* mode, staff and parent together should operate in *problem solving* mode that says, "How can we work this out?" or "Is there a compromise that we'll both be happy with?"

🐛 *how would you feel if you were a parent when . . .*

you don't know what is going on with your child during the day?

Give lots of information to parents, served in digestible portions, not all at once and not only one time. Information about what is happening, not just to their child but about the operation of the program, serves at least two purposes. The information itself is useful and/or interesting, but the message behind the message is, "This is your business. We have nothing to hide here; we expect you to want to know."

Systems of written communication can be an effective *supplement* to face-to-face communication with the teacher. However, guard against using written communication as a substitute for talking with parents.

🍎 *how would you feel if you were a parent when . . .*

you return at the end of the day and your child is off by himself, has a wet diaper, is roaming around aimlessly, or is just distressed?

It is not realistic, or possible for that matter, to ensure that every child is happy, clean, and constructively engaged upon the parent's return. Teachers, however, need to be sensitive to parents' impressions, and to do what they can with integrity to assure parents that their child is being well looked after. Parents differ in what their priorities are, and this is something that teachers will become more sensitive to as they get to know individual parents. For example, some parents value cleanliness much more than others.

❦ how would you feel if you were a parent when . . .

you believe that the teachers are more knowledgeable and expert about your child than you are?

Teachers are in a bit of a bind. While you aim high and try to present a professional image and assure parents that their young children are in good hands so that they will feel secure, you also want them to be involved, hang around, ask questions, and maintain their responsibility as the child's most important person. That is tricky.

The risk is that if you are too impressive, demonstrating competence and confidence, parents may very well trust and say, "I don't need to know what is going on." While that may be fine up to a point, it is dangerous, especially in child care, because of its impact on the parent-child relationship.

It is a challenge to convey what I call optimum certainty and confidence. On the one hand, you want to demonstrate to parents that you know what you are doing, but without implying that you are omniscient, as though you have all the answers and that if the child were yours, he or she would be perfect.

Competence on the part of early childhood professionals can lead to a feeling of less competence on the parents' part unless priority is given to forming partnerships.

🍎 *how would you feel if you were a parent when . . .*

you feel judged or criticized ?

While parents who use care almost universally say that they like to get good news about their child, hardly any parents say that they want unasked for advice about how to rear their child. Teachers need to exercise the utmost tact when making suggestions to parents about child rearing practices. One of the hardest things for many early childhood professionals to do is prioritize in importance their own values, beliefs, and preferences about what is good for children — in other words, to sort out what matters a lot and what matters less.

🍎 *how would you feel if you were a parent when . . .*

you are using care for the first time?

Parents using care for the first time don't know what is expected of them. They may not even know what questions to ask, and so staff should provide information even if parents don't ask. One of the roles of staff is to help new parents figure out what the staff expects from parents. They will be looking for cues and information about whether or not to stay around, whether or not their questions are welcomed or seen as a nuisance. While it is not realistic to think of handing out a definitive statement about *how to be a cool parent here,* teachers need to communicate over and over the message, "We want you here; we respect you. You are the most important person to your child; we want to know what you think, what you want." To help orient new parents, use others who have already settled in to share their *inside information.*

Many tensions are created by lack of clarity about what is expected, what is appropriate. This is a particular issue for family day care, where policies and practices in individual homes may not be spelled out and are likely to differ significantly among homes within a network. Efforts to help caregivers sort out what matters to them and what they expect of parents, and support to communicate that information effectively to parents, will bear fruit in enhanced relationships.

I suggest that this book be used with parents. Let parents read it, then discuss it with them. It is helpful to bring their hopes and insecurities out in the open, to validate them as legitimate and expected. Let them know that just as it is normal for *some* two year olds to bite, it is normal for *some* parents to have separation problems, or to feel unsure about whether or not they are doing the right thing leaving their child in care. A slight caution is in order, however: take care not to make the parent who does not feel guilty feel guilty because she doesn't!

A partnership begins with the first encounter the parent has with the center or family day care home. Impressions about openness of staff, ability to have input into decisions about their child, friendliness, and flexibility come from the beginning. Once the child begins, the settling in period is crucial for helping not only the child feel secure but also the parents.

Having welcomed parents and helped them settle in, however, it is critical that staff reinforce and maintain the initial welcome. Once is not enough. Initial messages of welcome will be made meaningful to parents only if they are demonstrated in daily interactions.

Keep trying.

🍎 *how would you feel if you were a parent when . . .*

you hear two different stories about the child's day or behavior?

Several issues are relevant here.

First, it is best if there is one consistent person or, if one is not possible, a few people to communicate with parents about their child.

Second, there is the issue of differing assessments by staff of the child's day or behavior. To some extent, this is inevitable, but staff must avoid such discrepant interpretations that parents question the honesty of the feedback given.

Third, staff may have different views about how much honesty is appropriate with parents. As with other differences in views of individual staff members, these differences, if not acknowledged and worked through, can undermine the effectiveness of the program. For the sake of consistency of approach, some compromise will be necessary to care for children as well as caring for relationships with parents.

It does undermine parents' feelings of confidence and security when they get conflicting information about their child. It is important for teachers to get their stories straight!

🐛 *how would you feel if you were a parent when . . .*

you and your child are more or less left alone by the staff during the settling in period?

The settling in period is a time for the teacher to become familiar with both parent and child through observation and discussion.

Just as important, of course, is that it is a time for both parent and child to get to know the teacher. This will not happen unless they interact, and the care and well being of the child is gradually *handed over* by the parent to the teacher.

Teachers, constantly busy with other children, should resist a tendency to overlook the new child as long as the parent is present.

🍎 *how would you feel if you were a parent when . . .*

**your child's special teacher is away
for an extended period of time?**

The absence of the child's special teacher can make both parent and child feel insecure, especially if the child is very young. Parents need to be told about planned absences ahead of time and reassured that there are others on the staff who know the child and are known well by the child. In family day care, assistance to make alternative arrangements during a provider's absence, and arrangements that allow parent and child to become familiar with the substitute, will help.

🍎 *how would you feel if you were a parent when . . .*

**the staff ask if they can make a home visit,
or they inform you that you need to let them know
if there is anything happening at home
and in the family that may affect
the child's behavior in care?**

As early childhood professionals, we may assume that we need to know, in fact that we have a right to know, what is going on in a family that may affect a child's behavior.

Jim Greenman (in press) describes a situation where a staff member shares with other staff that she has heard from a friend that a child's parents are separating. The reaction of the other staff is that it explains why the child has been acting up, and the staff express annoyance that the mother has not told them.

Greenman suggests that if that view is correct, then perhaps when things are going on in the staff's lives that affect their performance, we should send a note home to let parents know. Something like, "The children in Jane's group may behave differently at home because of problems with staff. There is considerable tension between Jane and her assistant (or Jane's marriage is splitting up, or Jane has a drinking problem). There have been some breaks in the routine and some tension, but don't worry because the program is still good and their on-the-job performance is still acceptable. Just please try and give your child some special attention because she may be feeling a bit insecure. We thought this information might help explain your child's behavior."

It is tempting to justify knowing all the details of a family's private life because it will help us *understand* or *teach* a child. But we have no right to know the ins and outs of family life, any more than parents have a right to know about our private lives as a means of monitoring program quality or gaining better understanding of the program. For the most part, what we need to know is that a child is under some unusual stress and needs us at our most supportive best. Much of the time, it makes little difference in our response whether the stress is due to family problems, fitful sleep, mild illness, or all the other sources of children's stress. What we do is try to offer flexibility, warmth, and nurturing. If a child is older, perhaps it may help the child to talk about the situation. But in that case, let the child or parent decide. Respect for parents demands that unless the situation is one of abuse or neglect, the parents control what information they wish to share. If we come to know something about the family, as professionals we should ask the parent if they mind before we share the information with colleagues or supervisors. A staff member discussing a family situation, based on gossip and without parental permission, is no less unprofessional than a group discussion about a teacher's private struggles.

5. not all parents are lovely

Not all staff are either, it must be said.

So far, this book may sound as though every parent who uses care is reasonable, responsible, rational, caring about their child, and sensitive. The vast majority are; but there are in every program a few parents who are difficult, critical, demanding, irresponsible, or uncooperative. These people test the professionalism of teachers, especially home based caregivers, where there is no relief and often no other adult present to provide support. With these parents, try to understand where the behavior may be coming from, what purpose it serves. For example, do they lack power in other areas of their life? What image do they have of themselves as people, as parents?

It is often those parents who behave in ways that are least likely to elicit support and help who are the ones most in need of it. For example, parents who are critical of staff and who make unreasonable demands may be uncertain about their skills as parents, and see this as a misguided way of demonstrating that they are good parents.

In the same way that it is nonsense for staff to act as though they enjoy all children equally, it is not possible, not human, in fact, to like all parents equally. In an atmosphere of professionalism, it should be acceptable for staff to talk about parents they have a hard time getting along with, parents they just can't warm up to.

Just as with children, the aim with parents is not to love them or even like them, but to respect them and to work with them on behalf of their children.

6. conclusion

So, in summary, what helps parents to feel comfortable and confident about leaving their child in care?

When they feel welcomed, known, accepted, and respected.

When they feel that their child is really known by, and really knows, the people who care for him or her.

When they are given lots of information about what is happening and are asked for their views.

When they are involved in making decisions about their child's experience.

When both they and their child are received and greeted upon arrival.

**When their child is
happy, secure,
and
engaged.**

**When they feel that
their child is not just
looked after but
cared for.**

**When everyone operates
with the understanding
that a kind word —
and a little support
and encouragement —
goes a long way.**

One of the great challenges facing early childhood professionals is how to let parents know how much they value a pat on the back and other signs of appreciation. Especially if parents know no other care, they may take what they have for granted. Similarly, staff should think about passing along anything they can genuinely say that is supportive and encouraging to parents.

A child care center director that I know put it well. She said that she works on helping her staff become attached, not to children, but to families. The challenge for early childhood professionals is to support parents in their child rearing role. To do this they must be clear themselves and make clear to parents the optimum relationship that should exist between parents and people who work with and teach their children. In order to do this, we have to advocate for policies that acknowledge the importance of partnerships with parents, and the complexity of establishing and maintaining those partnerships.

References and Resources

Caldwell, B. (1984). What is quality child care? *Young Children*, March, pp. 3-8.

Gonzalez-Mena, J. (2001). *Infants, Toddlers and Caregivers*. Mountain View, CA: Mayfield Publishing Company.

Greenman, J., & Stonehouse, A. (1996). *Prime Times: A Handbook for Excellence in Infant and Toddler Care*. St. Paul, MN: Redleaf Press.

Hendrick, J. (1988). *The Whole Child*, 4th Edition. Columbus, OH: Merrill.

Stonehouse, A. (1991). *Opening the Doors*. Canberra, Australia: Australian Early Childhood Association.

Warren, R. (1977). *Caring*. Washington, DC: National Association for the Education of Young Children.

Visit www.ChildCareExchange.com
for additional parenting articles.
Also available:
Parenting Exchange monthly e-newsletter and
Library of articles.

Also, visit the Australian Early Childhood Association:
www.aeca.org.au